This bite-sized book has been designed to give you a useful overview of how connecting with nature can boost your wellbeing and will help you to do the following:

- Understand nature
- Embrace
- Reduce your
- Invigorate your energy levels
- Appreciate the beauty of the world around you
- Connect responsibly and positively with the environment

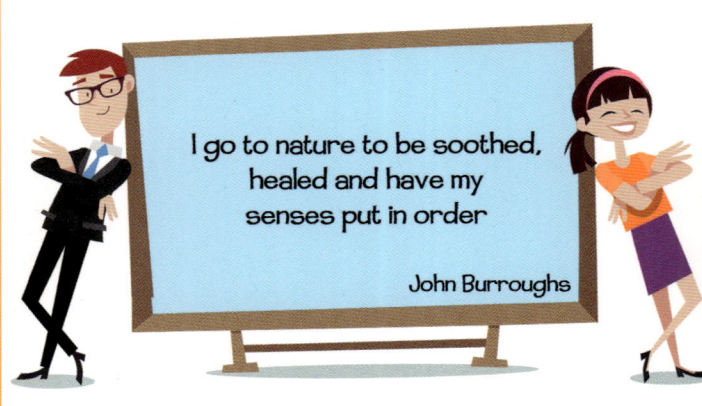

The power and beauty of nature

Nature underpins our economy, our society and our existence. Nature is free, and because of this we can often take it for granted and even overexploit it. Understanding the healing power of nature and taking time to appreciate its beauty is something that will help us to live happier, healthier and more fulfilling lives.

Our trees, rivers, oceans and soils provide us with the food we eat, the air we breathe and the water we irrigate our crops with. Nature performs major miracles for us every day of our lives so appreciating and respecting our environment is fundamental to our overall wellbeing.

Nature and wellbeing

The natural world is the foundation of our health, wellbeing and prosperity and exposure to nature is beneficial for all of us as human beings. Connecting to nature can boost our mental health and contribute to our physical wellbeing by reducing blood pressure, regulating heart rate, easing muscle tension and managing stress levels.

There are so many ways that we can bring nature into our everyday life from indoor or outdoor gardening, exercising in the fresh air, exploring green spaces and being around insects and animals. Any way that we can connect with nature will have a positive impact on our overall health and wellbeing.

Nature and ecotherapy

Ecotherapy, also known as nature therapy or green therapy, is the applied practice of the emergent field of ecopsychology which was originally developed by Theodore Roszak. Ecotherapy is a formal type of therapeutic treatment which involves doing outdoor activities in nature.

Ecotherapy can take place in both rural and urban settings, including parks, gardens, farms and woodlands. Usually it is led by a trained professional who is there to support and provide focus on doing an activity that takes place in a green environment. Ecotherapy can improve mental wellbeing, as well as encourage more physical activity and can help people who are lonely or socially isolated to broaden their networks.

Sensing nature

It can be truly wonderful to absorb ourselves in the whole sensory experience of nature using our five basic senses of touch, sight, hearing, smell and taste. The sensing organs associated with each of these send information to our brain which helps us to fully engage and understand the environment we are in. Some ways we sense nature may be as follows:

- Listening to the sound of birdsong
- Noticing the fluttering wings of butterflies
- Feeling the smoothness of a conker
- Tasting fresh fruit from the bushes and trees
- Smelling the perfume of flower blossom
- Feeling natural water against our skin
- Looking out for rainbows

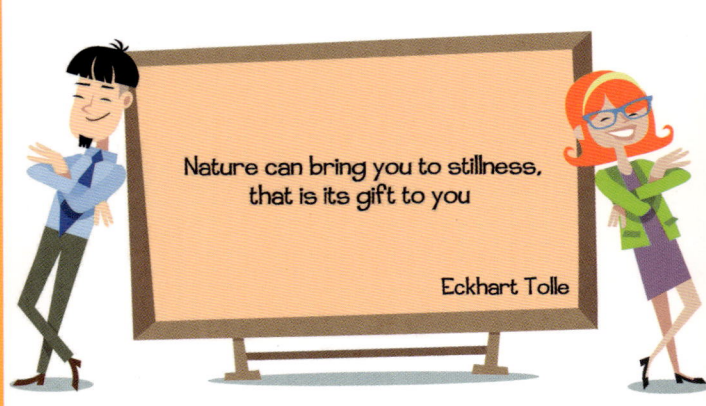

How to connect well with nature

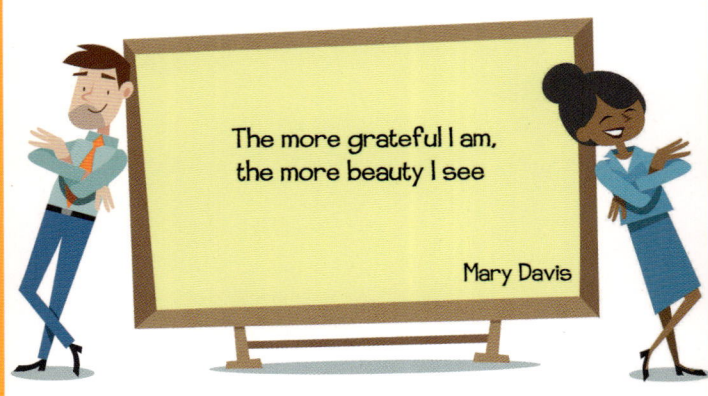

Be grateful for nature

We are living in the busy ages and often we have so much going on that we can take for granted the wonders of nature and what is happening around us in the actual moment. Being more mindful and creating intentional pauses in our day to notice and appreciate things is so important for our overall wellbeing.

When we take time each day to be grateful for what is happening around us, we will begin to appreciate things far more. Simply observing a beautiful butterfly feeding amongst the flowers in the garden, or listening to a bird singing, can bring with it a precious moment of joy.

Let the fresh air in

Opening our windows and doors allows natural air to flow through our homes which can provide a more relaxing and natural atmosphere. This also allows us to let out stale air because this is air that has been breathed in and doesn't contain as much oxygen as the fresh air from the outside.

A lack of fresh air can mean a lack of oxygen to the brain resulting in fatigue and dullness of mind. So, even on a cold day, turning off the central heating, wrapping up warm and letting some fresh air breeze through our homes can do us the world of good.

Do some gardening

Gardening is a fascinating experience that exposes us directly to the work of nature as we watch things grow. It has also been proven to improve mood, manage feelings of anxiety and depression as well as reduce stress levels.

Gardening is also a great way to get fit with digging and shovelling coming top of the list for burning the most calories and mowing and weeding not too far behind. Gardening can be a very creative activity and provides us with a sense of purpose and achievement, as well as inspiring us with the many miracles of nature.

Embrace indoor gardening

Indoor gardening can be rewarding in lots of ways and is becoming increasingly popular. It is a great way to spruce up our homes, and plants can keep us company and are a joy to be around. Pruning, watering, repotting and generally caring for our indoor garden can be calming and therapeutic.

Also, with the right amount of light, we can grow our delicious herbs, fruits and vegetables indoors or in window boxes. The added benefit is we get the opportunity to consume organic food which is great for our overall health and can save us money too. Some indoor plants, like peace lilies, can also purify the air so these also make great organic air fresheners.

Eat fresh foods

Eating food that is naturally grown and recently harvested is excellent for our health and wellbeing. The knowledge that our food was naturally produced will also allow us to savour each meal with a greater confidence in the ingredients.

As well as growing our own produce, where possible, shopping at a farmer's market can be a rewarding way to spend both time and money. It is also beneficial to understand the nutritional content of what we consume. This will help us to avoid eating processed foods, with high levels of refined carbohydrates and artificial additives, which can affect our overall health and mood.

Exercise outside

Walking is a great form of exercise and it is simple, free and one of the easiest ways to get more active, lose weight and boost our overall wellbeing. Whether we walk in the local park or around the neighbourhood, getting outside exposure will strengthen our connection with nature.

Walking 10,000 steps is equal to walking approximately five miles. This number of steps is often quoted as a good daily target to aim for and will help to boost our emotional and physical health. Any sport or hobby that involves the great outdoors is an excellent way to get our exercise.

Embrace forest bathing

Forest bathing means taking in, through all of our senses, the forest atmosphere. It is the conscious and contemplative practice of being fully immersed in the sights, sounds and smells of the forest.

There are over 60,000 tree species in the world and they contribute to our environment by providing oxygen, improving air quality, conserving water, preserving soil and supporting wildlife. See how many trees you can name the next time you go for a walk.

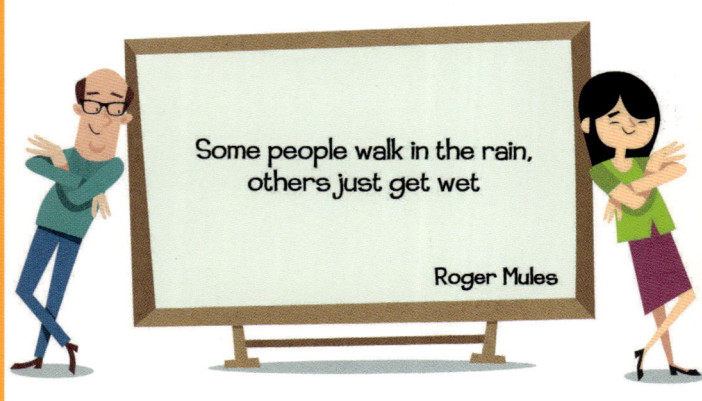

Walk in the rain

Scientific studies have shown that the air is cleaner during and after heavy rainfall. This is because when raindrops fall through the atmosphere, they attract hundreds of particles of pollutants before hitting the ground. So, invigorating breaths of rainy air can stimulate our senses.

Rain also helps to improve the health of our hair and skin so collecting rain water to bath in occasionally can be a lovely natural treat. Also, walking in the rain helps to burn more calories as we tend to walk at a faster pace so this can reduce body fat and make us healthier.

Visit bodies of water

Brain imaging research has shown that proximity to water is strongly linked to our brains releasing feel-good hormones, including dopamine and oxytocin. Water is the fundamental basis of all life on earth and natural bodies of water can be so beautiful.

Whether it is sitting peacefully by a lake, river or stream or walking along the beach listening to the sound of the waves, the naturally soothing effect of water can be profound. Wild swimming in natural bodies of water has been linked to reducing stress levels and enhancing happiness.

Go camping

A camping trip on our own, or with friends and family, can be a wonderful way to bond not only with each other but also with nature. Getting away from technology and the noise of everyday life and being amongst the trees and stars can be so relaxing.

Imagine a day filled with exploring the countryside and nature, followed by an evening of great conversation and stories whilst sitting around a campfire toasting something delicious. Then far away from the city lights, falling to sleep beneath a pure pitch-black sky filled with sparkling stars. Bliss!

Stargaze

When we look at the sky on a clear evening, we will be able to see a few thousand individual stars with our naked eye and even with a modest amateur telescope, millions more will come into view. NASA estimates that there are about 100 billion stars in our galaxy; however, to establish the exact amount would be like trying to count grains of sand on a beach.

Stargazing can connect us with nature as we gaze in awe at the vastness of the star filled sky. The best time to go stargazing is the days before, during and soon after each new moon. This is when we will be able to see far more of those magical stars with our naked eye.

Appreciate the value of insects

According to the Royal Entomological Society there are over one million species of insects that have been discovered and described; however, it is estimated that there may be as many as 10 million species on earth.

Insect behaviour is fascinating and these little creatures provide very useful services to mankind and the environment, in so many ways. Insects keep pest insects in check, pollinate crops and act as sanitation experts by cleaning up waste so that the world doesn't become overrun with dung!

Notice each season's flowers

Flowers can have an immediate impact on our happiness and a long-term positive effect on our mood. Various studies have reported people feeling less depressed, anxious and agitated after receiving flowers.

Flowers can provide natural medicines for humans and some animals and they also assist in a plant's reproduction by attracting outside pollinators. Without all the varied colours of flowers, plants would only be green, and the world would be a duller place. Noticing each flower that is in season and learning their names is a great way to exercise our minds as we learn about each one.

Spend time around animals

It takes just a few minutes of playing with animals to feel less anxious and stressed. This is because cortisol, the hormone associated with stress, is lowered and serotonin, the chemical associated with happiness, is boosted. Interacting with animals has all been proven to help with depression and combat feelings of isolation.

Various research has also identified that even watching nature programmes can boost our mood and make us feel better.

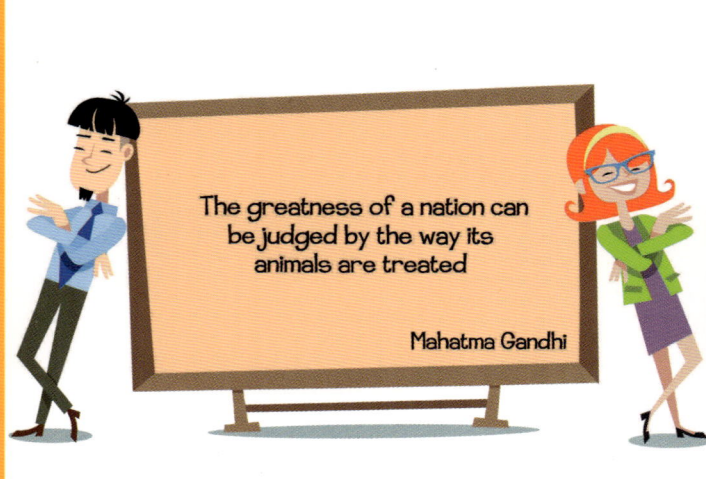

Protect and support wildlife

To maintain a healthy ecological balance on earth, animals, marine species and plants are as important as human beings. Every organism has a unique function in the food chain that makes a valuable contribution to our ecosystem. Many animals and birds are becoming endangered. So, by conserving wildlife, we are ensuring that futuree generations can enjoy our natural world and all the important species that live within it.

Learning more about wildlife, living responsibly, volunteering and making donations can all be so helpful. Adopting an animal for someone, as a special gift, is just one wonderful way that will help people feel that they are doing their bit for the environment.

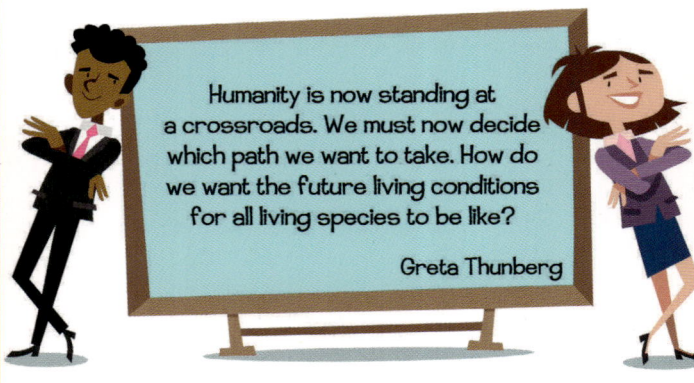

> Humanity is now standing at a crossroads. We must now decide which path we want to take. How do we want the future living conditions for all living species to be like?
>
> Greta Thunberg

Be kind to the planet

If we all make the effort to reduce our impact on the environment, then together, we can make a positive difference. The changes that we make don't have to be huge either and there are so many simple things that we can do at home or in the workplace that will help. Making a conscious habit of eliminating one-use plastic, saving water, turning off lights or thinking twice before we drive our cars, instead of cycling or walking, can make such an important impact.

These actions will positively contribute towards reducing factors such as carbon emissions and greenhouse gases, as well as saving us money. We will also be richer in the knowledge that we are eco warriors rather than an eco wreckers!

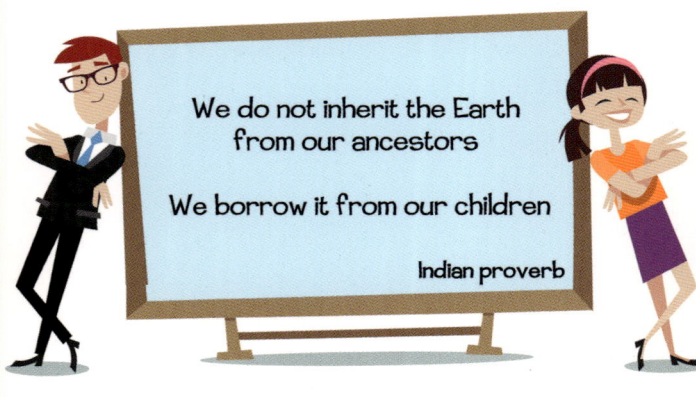